I0013492

AI IN CONSTRUCTION

AI Tools for Smarter, Safer Construction

by Sayeed Siddiqui

Copyright Page

Copyright © 2025 by Sayeed Siddiqui
 All rights reserved. No part of this book may be reproduced, stored in a retrieval system, or transmitted in any form by any means—electronic, mechanical, photocopying, recording, or otherwise—without prior written permission from the author, except in the case of brief quotations used in articles or reviews.

Published by: [Your Publishing Imprint or Self-Publishing Platform]
Contact: **supreme.clarion@gmail.com**
First Edition: 2025
ISBN: [To be assigned]
Cover Design by: [Your Name or Designer]
Printed in [Your Country]

Dedication

To all the masons, architects, planners, and
engineers who shaped the past,
 And to the pioneers who will build the
future—with data, code, and vision.
 Dedicated also to Arpita Arya—your
wisdom and brilliance inspire every blueprint
of my imagination.

Table of Contents

Introduction

The world is being rebuilt—and not just in bricks and mortar. A technological transformation is rippling through every steel beam and cement slab, a transformation led by Artificial Intelligence.

AI is not the future of construction—it is the present. From towering skyscrapers in smart cities to sustainable residential communities, AI is changing how we design, plan, build, maintain, and think about construction. For some, it means streamlined workflows and better productivity. For others, it signals disruption, requiring urgent upskilling. But for all, it presents an opportunity—one that must be understood, embraced, and wielded wisely.

This book, *AI in Construction*, is written for:

- **Contractors** seeking to streamline operations

- **Architects and designers** exploring generative and parametric modeling

- **Project managers** aiming to reduce delays and cost overruns

- **Engineers** interested in real-time monitoring and predictive analytics

- **Students and newcomers** aiming to understand what lies ahead

- **Small business owners** who think AI is only for the big players

- **Policymakers and consultants** crafting the infrastructure of tomorrow

In the coming pages, we explore how machine learning, robotics, computer vision, natural language processing, and other AI applications are being adopted in construction—from planning and safety to material handling and post-construction asset management.

This is not just a technical manual or a research overview. It is a **comprehensive, real-world guide**—backed by examples, case studies, and a practical tone—designed to empower you to make informed decisions and strategic shifts in your work.

As the global population urbanizes and demands for housing, infrastructure, and smart cities grow, the construction sector must evolve rapidly to meet challenges of cost, climate, safety, and speed.

Let this book be your blueprint for that evolution.

Chapter 1: The Digital Blueprint – AI's Arrival in Construction

The Changing Landscape of Construction

For centuries, construction has been the cornerstone of human civilization. From the pyramids of Egypt to the skyscrapers of modern metropolises, it has reflected the values, technology, and ambition of each era. Yet, for all its grandeur, the construction industry has long been one of the slowest to adopt digital innovation—relying on manual labor, paper-based planning, and legacy methods well into the 21st century.

But times are changing—and fast. A seismic shift is underway.

Enter Artificial Intelligence (AI): a technology once confined to science fiction, now at the heart of almost every modern industry. In construction, it is redefining what's possible—from how buildings are designed to how job sites are managed. With AI, the construction industry now has the tools to increase efficiency, reduce errors, improve safety, and enhance sustainability on a scale never before imagined.

This chapter lays the foundation. It is the **digital blueprint**—a comprehensive look at how and why AI is transforming the construction industry and what this means for professionals at every level.

1.1 Understanding Artificial Intelligence in Simple Terms

At its core, **Artificial Intelligence** refers to machines programmed to mimic human cognitive functions such as learning, reasoning, problem-solving, and perception. AI systems can analyze large volumes of data, recognize patterns, make decisions, and even learn from outcomes to improve future performance.

In construction, this translates into:

- Machines that can read blueprints and suggest optimizations

- Algorithms that forecast project delays or safety risks

- Drones that map job sites in real-time with centimeter-level accuracy

- Robots that lay bricks, tie rebar, or pour concrete

- Smart systems that adjust HVAC based on real-time occupancy and weather data

And this is just the beginning.

1.2 Why the Construction Industry is Ripe for AI Disruption

According to a McKinsey report, the global construction industry contributes nearly **$10 trillion** to the world economy but suffers from **low productivity growth**—ranking just above agriculture. In some markets, construction projects routinely go **80% over budget and 20% over schedule**.

These inefficiencies stem from:

- Fragmented supply chains

- Poor project planning

- Labor shortages

- Safety incidents and costly rework

- Lack of digitization

AI is not a luxury—it is a necessity. It can address many of these challenges head-on by introducing **data-driven decision-making**, real-time monitoring, predictive insights, and automated task execution.

1.3 Historical Resistance to Change

Despite its benefits, the construction industry has traditionally been slow to embrace new technologies. This resistance comes from several factors:

- High upfront costs

- Lack of digital literacy

- Fear of job displacement

- Complex stakeholder ecosystems

- Regulatory and compliance barriers

However, recent global events—including the COVID-19 pandemic and climate-driven disasters—have exposed vulnerabilities in traditional construction methods and **accelerated the urgency for digital transformation**.

Today, leading construction firms are investing heavily in AI-powered technologies to stay competitive—and those that fail to adapt may not survive the next decade.

1.4 Key Drivers Behind AI Adoption in Construction

The rapid growth of AI in construction is being driven by a confluence of factors:

1.4.1 Data Explosion

Construction sites now generate vast amounts of data from drones, sensors, cameras, wearables, BIM models, and software platforms. AI makes it possible to analyze this data in real-time and turn it into actionable insights.

1.4.2 Labor Shortage

Skilled labor is in short supply in many markets. AI-enabled robotics and automation can fill this gap without compromising quality or speed.

1.4.3 Safety Concerns

Construction is one of the most dangerous professions. AI can predict safety risks before they happen, enabling proactive measures that save lives.

1.4.4 Sustainability Goals

Green building is no longer optional. AI helps optimize energy use, reduce material waste, and monitor emissions, aligning projects with environmental targets.

1.4.5 Cost and Time Pressures

Clients and governments demand faster delivery at lower cost. AI-driven scheduling, procurement, and site management tools dramatically reduce delays and overruns.

1.5 Major Applications of AI in Construction

Let's examine some of the core ways AI is already being applied on construction projects today:

1.5.1 AI in Design (BIM + Generative Design)

AI can analyze thousands of design permutations using algorithms to suggest the most cost-effective and structurally sound options. Integrated with **Building Information Modeling (BIM)**, it ensures designs are optimized even before ground is broken.

1.5.2 Planning and Scheduling

AI tools can create dynamic schedules that adapt in real-time to changing conditions—such as weather delays or material shortages. They learn from past projects to improve future planning accuracy.

1.5.3 Risk Management and Safety

By analyzing past incident reports, sensor data, and worker behavior, AI systems can identify risk hotspots, predict accidents, and flag non-compliance with safety protocols.

1.5.4 Autonomous Construction Equipment

From excavators to bulldozers, AI is enabling **autonomous or semi-autonomous vehicles** on-site, reducing reliance on human drivers and operators.

1.5.5 Quality Control

Computer vision algorithms can inspect work as it's being done—comparing real-time images with BIM models to detect defects, measure tolerances, or identify progress deviations.

1.6 Case Studies: AI in Action

Let's briefly look at real-world examples showing AI's impact:

Case 1: Vinci Construction, France

Using AI-powered scheduling software, Vinci reduced project delays by over 25% on large infrastructure projects by dynamically reallocating resources and predicting bottlenecks.

Case 2: Skanska USA

Implemented AI-based safety analytics using wearables and cameras to reduce on-site injuries by 30% in high-risk environments.

Case 3: ICON, USA

This company uses robotic 3D printing guided by AI to build low-cost homes in just 24 hours—revolutionizing affordable housing in disaster-prone and underserved regions.

1.7 Small Firms, Big Opportunities

One of the biggest misconceptions about AI is that it is only for large corporations with deep pockets. In reality, cloud-based AI tools and open-source platforms have made it accessible even to **small and medium-sized contractors**.

Apps for estimating, automated bidding, client communication, remote inspections, and energy efficiency calculations are available at low cost—often with free tiers. This democratization of AI means small builders can now **compete with larger players** by being agile, innovative, and data-savvy.

1.8 Challenges and Considerations

While the potential of AI is immense, its adoption comes with challenges:

- **Data Privacy**: Handling large volumes of sensitive site data must be governed by strict security protocols.

- **Integration with Legacy Systems**: AI tools must work seamlessly with existing software and workflows.

- **Bias and Transparency**: AI models trained on biased data can yield flawed outcomes, requiring careful oversight.

- **Training and Upskilling**: The current workforce must be upskilled to use new technologies effectively and ethically.

1.9 The Road Ahead

The journey of AI in construction has just begun. As hardware becomes cheaper, algorithms become more powerful, and 5G connectivity enables real-time remote collaboration, we will see even greater breakthroughs:

- Construction sites monitored entirely by drones

- AI-generated blueprints adapting in real-time to materials and labor availability

- Augmented reality overlays powered by machine learning

- Circular economy planning where waste from one site becomes input for another

In short, **AI is not a tool—it is a partner** in the building process.

Conclusion: Laying the Foundation

AI's arrival in construction is not a distant possibility—it is happening now. As we move deeper into this book, we'll explore specific AI applications, tools, and strategies across every phase of the construction lifecycle.

From concept to commissioning, AI offers a competitive edge, a safety net, and a path to sustainable growth.

The question is no longer "Should we use AI in construction?"
 The question is, "How fast can we adapt—and how well will we build the future?"

Let's move to **Chapter 2: Smart Design and Architecture with Generative AI**—where the blueprint meets the algorithm.

Chapter 2: Smart Design and Architecture with Generative AI

The New Era of Intelligent Design

Design has always been the soul of construction. It's where imagination takes shape—on paper, screen, or in a digital model—before a single brick is laid. But today, architecture and structural design are undergoing a profound transformation driven by Artificial Intelligence, particularly through a technique called **Generative Design**.

This chapter explores how AI enables a smarter, faster, and more adaptive design process, allowing architects, engineers, and developers to collaborate with machines that *learn*, *create*, and *optimize* like never before.

2.1 What Is Generative Design?

Generative Design is an iterative design process that uses AI algorithms to explore a vast number of design permutations—based on defined constraints like materials, cost, dimensions, site limitations, structural integrity, and environmental impact.

You tell the software:

- Here are the goals (e.g., minimize material cost)

- Here are the rules (e.g., must support X load, stay within Y height)

- And the AI does the rest—generating thousands of optimized solutions in seconds

This technology moves beyond static blueprints and introduces **living models** that learn from each iteration, getting better as they go.

2.2 The Role of AI in Modern Architecture

Traditionally, architectural planning is a manual and time-consuming endeavor. Architects balance aesthetics, compliance, function, and feasibility. But with AI, they gain a powerful co-creator.

AI now enables:

- **Automated floor plan generation** based on zoning laws, sun orientation, and flow patterns

- **Optimization of building shapes** for energy efficiency, acoustics, and airflow

- **Cost-conscious material selection** that meets structural and aesthetic goals

- **Parametric modeling** that adjusts dynamically to site changes

- **Real-time 3D visualization** integrated with environmental simulations

Architects no longer need to pick between design *speed* and design *quality*—AI delivers both.

2.3 How Generative AI Works in Construction

Generative AI follows a simple yet powerful feedback loop:

1. **Input Parameters**: Constraints and goals are defined (cost, material, size, load-bearing limits, etc.)

2. **Algorithmic Generation**: AI generates thousands of design permutations

3. **Simulation & Analysis**: Structural stress, energy efficiency, airflow, and spatial use are analyzed

4. **Ranking Solutions**: AI ranks solutions by performance against desired criteria

5. **Human Refinement**: Designers select the best candidates for further refinement

It's a **co-evolution** between human intuition and machine precision.

2.4 Case Study: Autodesk's Project Refinery

Autodesk, a leader in design software, introduced **Project Refinery**—a generative design tool integrated with **Revit**, its BIM software. One real-world example involved designing a new office layout for their Toronto headquarters.

- Over **10,000 layout options** were generated based on daylight, acoustic preferences, employee workflows, and seating preferences.

- Final design improved **natural lighting** by 20%, **acoustic comfort** by 30%, and **workflow efficiency** by 22%.

Such gains would take human designers weeks, if not months, to achieve manually.

2.5 AI and BIM: A Perfect Marriage

Building Information Modeling (BIM) has already revolutionized construction documentation by allowing 3D, data-rich digital representations of physical structures.

AI adds intelligence to BIM by:

- **Auto-detecting clashes** between building systems

- **Predicting cost overruns** based on historic data

- **Improving coordination** across stakeholders in real time

- **Suggesting sustainable materials** based on lifecycle analysis

- **Simulating human movement** through a space for safety and convenience

With AI, BIM evolves from a *visual model* to a *thinking partner*—one that advises and evolves.

2.6 Environmental Design and Net-Zero Buildings

Sustainability is no longer optional in modern construction. Generative AI is now key to **net-zero energy building** design. It can analyze:

- Solar orientation and shadow paths

- Heat gain and loss across surfaces

- Wind flow and ventilation

- Optimal placement of green walls, windows, and insulation

- Lifecycle carbon footprint of materials

For example, AI can suggest:

- Rotating the building by 15 degrees to reduce HVAC load by 18%

- Using phase-changing materials to absorb heat

- Planting vertical gardens to improve insulation and biodiversity

This level of precision ensures buildings are both high-performing and environmentally responsible.

2.7 Small Firms Can Use It Too

One misconception about generative AI tools is that they're too expensive or complex for small firms. But several **affordable or open-source tools** exist:

- **TestFit.io** – Quickly generate site and building layouts based on real-world constraints

- **Spacemaker AI (Autodesk)** – For urban planning, light and noise simulations

- **Hypar** – Offers modular generative design tools for developers and architects

- **Grasshopper + Rhino** – Parametric modeling with open-source plug-ins for AI features

With access to cloud computing, even modest design studios can generate powerful outputs once reserved for global consultancies.

2.8 Augmented Creativity: Architects + AI = Genius

AI is not replacing architects. It is **augmenting** their creativity.

A good analogy is music composition. AI can compose technically perfect melodies, but a human adds soul. Likewise, AI can suggest 100 building layouts, but only an architect understands human culture, emotion, and context to make the final call.

This human-machine collaboration allows architects to:

- Explore bold ideas without wasting time

- Test constraints instantly

- Visualize "what-if" scenarios at scale

- Take greater creative risks backed by data

In essence, AI **frees humans from the repetitive**, allowing them to focus on innovation.

2.9 AI-Enhanced Design Thinking for Urban Spaces

Beyond individual buildings, AI is also being used to plan **entire neighborhoods and cities**. It takes into account:

- Traffic flow patterns

- Noise pollution and green space ratios

- Accessibility for elderly or disabled residents

- Density vs. livability balance

- Resilience to flood, fire, or climate risks

Urban planners are using AI simulations to reimagine **climate-resilient cities** with distributed energy systems, optimized pedestrian paths, and AI-monitored infrastructure.

2.10 Risks and Ethical Considerations

As with any powerful tool, AI in design must be wielded responsibly. Some key concerns include:

- **Design Bias**: AI trained on flawed data may perpetuate inequities (e.g., poor access in minority communities)

- **Loss of Craft**: Over-reliance may reduce traditional design skills

- **Data Dependency**: AI is only as good as the data fed into it—garbage in, garbage out

- **Creativity Ceiling**: AI is great at optimization, but not (yet) at raw inspiration or storytelling

- **Intellectual Property Issues**: Who owns an AI-generated blueprint?

These concerns require new codes of ethics and regulations to ensure AI enhances rather than diminishes the human touch in architecture.

2.11 The Near Future: Living Buildings and Smart Adaptation

Looking ahead, AI will not only **design** buildings—it will help them **adapt** in real time:

- Windows that adjust tint based on daylight

- HVAC that responds to occupancy and air quality

- Walls that absorb pollution and generate power

- Smart lighting that follows people to reduce energy use

- AI that *recommends renovations* over time as usage patterns change

Buildings will become **intelligent systems** that learn, evolve, and self-improve—blurring the line between static architecture and living organisms.

Conclusion: The Rise of the Algorithmic Architect

We are entering the age of the algorithmic architect—where machines assist in ideation, calculation, and optimization, while humans remain at the creative and ethical core.

Generative AI is not about removing the designer from the equation. It's about **amplifying the designer's ability** to create better spaces, faster, and more affordably—without compromising vision.

As we move to Chapter 3, we explore how AI transforms the next crucial stage: **Project Planning and Scheduling**—where time, cost, and coordination are reimagined by intelligent systems.

Chapter 3: AI in Project Planning and Scheduling

The Beating Heart of Construction: Time, Cost, and Coordination

If design is the soul of a construction project, then **planning and scheduling** are its heart. Without a coherent plan, even the most brilliant design can turn into chaos on-site. Yet, project delays, budget overruns, and poor coordination are shockingly common in construction.

A recent KPMG global survey revealed that only **25% of construction projects** came within 10% of their original deadlines. With millions lost to inefficiencies, AI is now stepping in—not as a tool, but as a *strategic partner*—to overhaul how projects are planned, sequenced, budgeted, and delivered.

This chapter shows how AI reshapes every phase of planning and scheduling, from early cost estimation to daily workforce management, unlocking precision, foresight, and control never before possible.

3.1 Traditional Planning Pitfalls

Construction projects are notoriously complex, involving multiple stakeholders—clients, architects, engineers, contractors, subcontractors, suppliers, and local authorities. Even small misalignments lead to delays, cost spikes, and legal disputes.

Common issues include:

- Over-reliance on static Gantt charts and spreadsheets

- Inaccurate time and cost estimations

- Resource misallocation

- Weather and site condition unpredictability

- Poor communication across teams

These challenges aren't just human—they're systemic. Traditional tools can't process the immense data generated during a project's lifecycle. That's where AI changes the game.

3.2 How AI Transforms Project Planning

AI brings two revolutionary advantages:

1. **Learning from history** – AI learns patterns from past projects to predict outcomes

2. **Real-time adjustment** – AI adapts to ongoing changes and updates the plan accordingly

This enables AI to:

- Predict risks before they happen

- Suggest optimal sequences of activities

- Reallocate resources instantly to avoid downtime

- Simulate various "what-if" scenarios

- Reduce manual oversight and paperwork

Think of it as a **self-healing construction plan**—responsive, adaptive, and intelligent.

3.3 AI in Cost Estimation and Budgeting

Before a shovel hits the ground, budgets must be defined. Traditionally, estimators rely on past experience, spreadsheets, and vendor quotes. AI, however, can:

- **Analyze thousands of cost benchmarks** from prior projects

- **Factor in inflation, labor rates, material availability**, and even **market sentiment**

- Use **Natural Language Processing (NLP)** to parse and learn from historical contracts, tenders, and RFQs

- **Update estimates in real time** as plans evolve or material prices change

Tools like **ProEst, Cleopatra Enterprise**, and **ALICE Technologies** use AI for smarter cost planning that adapts continuously, rather than staying fixed and obsolete.

3.4 Intelligent Scheduling with AI

AI-driven scheduling is **non-linear**, dynamic, and data-rich.

Instead of just mapping tasks, it:

- Optimizes **task dependencies and sequencing**

- Accounts for **machine availability**, **worker productivity**, and **site logistics**

- Simulates **delay impacts** (e.g., what happens if rebar delivery is late?)

- Learns from previous projects to avoid recurring bottlenecks

- Integrates with **BIM models** to visualize progress spatially

Example: AI might detect that pouring concrete in Zone B before waterproofing Zone A creates delays, then propose an alternate sequence to finish two days earlier.

3.5 Machine Learning for Risk Prediction

Every project has hidden landmines: weather disruptions, supply chain issues, regulatory delays, or safety incidents. With AI:

- Historical risk databases are analyzed to assign **probability scores** to risk events

- Early warning systems flag anomalies (e.g., sudden absenteeism of key crews)

- Geospatial AI uses weather data, traffic patterns, or site sensor info to forecast interruptions

- "Risk heatmaps" guide site managers to focus efforts where they're needed most

AI doesn't just report risks—it **anticipates and proposes mitigations** before they escalate.

3.6 Dynamic Resource Allocation

AI excels at matching the right people, equipment, and materials to the right task at the right time.

It considers:

- Crew availability and skills

- Machine usage hours

- Material lead times

- Site congestion levels

- Real-time delays

The system adapts daily schedules based on actual progress, much like a GPS re-routing you when there's traffic. No more idle workers waiting for deliveries or bottlenecks of overlapping subcontractors.

3.7 AI + BIM: Real-Time 4D and 5D Planning

When AI integrates with **4D BIM** (3D + time) and **5D BIM** (3D + time + cost), a new dimension of visibility emerges.

Planners can:

- Visualize how the schedule unfolds across the physical space

- Monitor cost implications of every task in real-time

- Simulate different timelines and their financial trade-offs

- Automatically generate procurement schedules aligned with the master plan

For example, moving the window installation earlier might increase scaffolding costs but allow earlier weatherproofing—AI evaluates this trade-off instantly.

3.8 Case Study: Mortenson Construction

Mortenson, a U.S. construction giant, used **ALICE Technologies** (an AI-powered scheduling engine) for a data center build.

- AI analyzed over 6 million possible schedules

- Proposed alternatives that reduced project duration by 17%

- Identified risky sequences that human planners missed

- Adjusted in real time to labor and delivery setbacks

This demonstrates how AI can outperform even experienced project managers in complex scheduling scenarios—especially when speed and cost savings are critical.

3.9 Weather Forecasting and Scenario Simulation

AI uses historical and real-time weather data to suggest:

- Ideal days for concrete curing or roof work

- Shutdown periods during heavy winds or storms

- Re-sequencing tasks to maintain progress despite rain forecasts

Advanced models simulate "what-if" scenarios:

- What happens if a strike delays rebar delivery by 4 days?

- How to fast-track tasks if client requests early delivery?

- How does a crane breakdown on Day 15 ripple through the schedule?

AI doesn't just answer "what"—it tells you "what to do about it."

3.10 Integrating AI with Project Management Software

AI is now embedded in tools like:

- **PlanGrid** (autofill data fields from photos and site reports)

- **Buildertrend** (predictive scheduling and client comms)

- **Procore** (automated analytics dashboards)

- **nPlan** (machine learning from global projects to predict delays)

- **OpenSpace** (AI-generated 360° progress tracking)

These tools don't replace your project managers—but they **supercharge their efficiency**, freeing them from routine tasks to focus on decision-making and leadership.

3.11 AI for Subcontractor Management

AI can monitor subcontractor performance over time:

- Were they consistently on time?

- Did their work require rework?

- Were there safety incidents linked to their crews?

This enables **data-driven contractor selection**, performance-based incentives, and early warnings when a subcontractor falls behind.

It also automates milestone payments by verifying actual progress via drones, cameras, and IoT sensors—avoiding disputes and delays.

3.12 Challenges to AI Adoption in Planning

Despite its potential, integrating AI into planning workflows faces hurdles:

- **Data Quality**: AI needs structured, clean data—rare in fragmented projects

- **Resistance to Change**: Veteran planners may distrust machine suggestions

- **Integration Costs**: Linking AI tools with legacy ERP, HR, or procurement systems

- **Real-Time Data Access**: Many decisions still rely on incomplete or delayed site data

Overcoming these requires a mix of **culture shift**, **training**, and **phased implementation**—starting with hybrid human-AI planning and gradually increasing automation.

3.13 Small Firms and AI Planning Tools

AI isn't just for billion-dollar megaprojects. Cloud-based planning platforms now offer AI-lite tools for small contractors:

- **SmartBid**: Automates bid management

- **Buildxact**: Uses AI for accurate residential estimates

- **Fonn**: Lightweight AI planning and field collaboration for SMEs

- **Monday.com Construction Templates**: With machine learning-based automation

These tools offer affordability, mobile compatibility, and ease of use—leveling the playing field for firms with fewer resources.

3.14 The Human Role: From Scheduler to Strategist

Far from making people obsolete, AI shifts the role of planners and PMs:

From → To
 Scheduler → Strategic Orchestrator
 Estimator → Risk-Focused Analyst
 Supervisor → Insight-Driven Leader
 Timekeeper → Dynamic Decision-Maker

AI handles the complexity. **Humans provide judgment, context, and trust**. Together, they form a planning brain no single entity can match.

Conclusion: A Smarter Way to Build

AI is redefining construction planning as we know it—from **predictive budgeting**, **autonomous scheduling**, and **risk-aware sequencing** to **real-time optimization** and **data-informed decision-making**.

Those who embrace this revolution will:

- Deliver projects faster and safer

- Win more competitive bids

- Reduce stress and miscommunication

- Scale efficiently with fewer surprises

As we progress to **Chapter 4: Predictive Maintenance and Safety with Machine Learning**, we will explore how AI goes beyond planning—protecting your people, machines, and investments in real-time.

Chapter 4: Predictive Maintenance and Safety with Machine Learning

Introduction: The Cost of Downtime and Danger

Construction is an industry where the stakes are high and the margins can be tight. Equipment breakdowns and safety incidents don't just cause delays—they can result in injury, lawsuits, material loss, and even death.

Globally, the construction industry is among the top sectors for workplace fatalities. Simultaneously, equipment failure accounts for **20–30%** of total project delays. In such an environment, proactive strategies are not just useful—they're essential.

Machine learning (ML)—a powerful subset of AI—is now being leveraged to *predict*, *prevent*, and *protect* across job sites. This chapter explores how ML algorithms are transforming reactive safety and maintenance systems into proactive guardians of both machinery and human life.

4.1 What is Predictive Maintenance?

Predictive maintenance (PdM) uses **data from sensors, usage logs, and environmental conditions** to predict when a machine is likely to fail—allowing proactive service to be done *before* the failure occurs.

Traditional maintenance types:

- **Reactive** – fix when it breaks

- **Preventive** – schedule fixes based on time

- **Predictive** – fix based on data signals and risk analysis

AI-powered PdM detects subtle anomalies in operation, such as:

- Overheating in excavator hydraulics

- Unusual vibration in crane motors

- Decline in fuel efficiency or hydraulic pressure

The result? Lower downtime, fewer emergency repairs, and longer equipment life.

4.2 How Machine Learning Works in Maintenance

Machine learning models are trained on large datasets of:

- Equipment performance under normal and failure conditions

- Maintenance logs and repair history

- Environmental factors like temperature and humidity

- Operator behavior (e.g., frequency of use, overloading, misuse)

These models detect **patterns invisible to humans**, such as:

- Early signs of engine wear

- Power fluctuations preceding a motor failure

- Minor deviations in operating rhythm that precede part breakdown

The system then issues:

- **Risk scores** for each asset

- **Recommended maintenance windows**

- **Spare part forecasts** and procurement schedules

4.3 Common Equipment Covered by Predictive AI

- **Excavators and Loaders**: Track hydraulic systems, undercarriage stress

- **Cranes**: Monitor cable tension, gearbox temperature

- **Concrete Mixers**: Analyze rotational patterns and drum efficiency

- **Pavers and Rollers**: Track vibrations, asphalt temperature ranges

- **Generators and Compressors**: Monitor pressure, oil quality, and runtime

These systems often use **Internet of Things (IoT) sensors** combined with AI to feed continuous data into centralized dashboards.

4.4 Benefits of Predictive Maintenance

- **Reduced Downtime**: AI identifies issues early, allowing time for repairs without stopping the site

- **Cost Savings**: Avoid costly breakdowns, emergency repairs, and overtime pay

- **Inventory Optimization**: Only order spare parts when needed, not by guesswork

- **Extended Equipment Life**: Consistent monitoring reduces wear and tear

- **Fewer Project Delays**: Equipment is available when scheduled

Example: A construction firm using AI noticed a 22% increase in uptime for heavy equipment by acting on early alerts for coolant leaks and belt issues.

4.5 Predictive Safety: From Reaction to Prevention

Now let's talk safety. Traditional safety systems are based on:

- Toolbox talks

- Compliance checklists

- Incident investigations (after the fact)

AI flips this model by *predicting incidents before they happen*. Using real-time data, AI can warn of:

- Worker fatigue based on activity data

- Unsafe scaffolding use detected by computer vision

- Unauthorized zone access using geofencing and wearables

- Unsafe equipment speeds or stress

This proactive approach can save lives—and billions.

4.6 Computer Vision for Safety Monitoring

Computer vision is AI's ability to "see" and interpret camera footage. When applied to safety:

- **Detect PPE compliance** (e.g., helmet, vest, gloves)

- **Flag unsafe behavior**, like leaning over edges or improper machine operation

- **Alert for crowding** in high-risk areas

- **Track material stacking risks** that may lead to toppling

Systems like **Smartvid.io**, **Indus.ai**, and **Everguard.ai** use AI models trained on thousands of site videos to detect unsafe scenarios in real time—often faster than human supervisors.

4.7 Wearables and Smart Safety Gear

Workers now wear AI-enhanced gear such as:

- **Smart Helmets**: Monitor head position, detect falls

- **Safety Vests**: Contain GPS for location tracking and heart rate sensors

- **Boot Sensors**: Detect sudden movements or abnormal gait

- **Smart Glasses**: Provide augmented safety instructions and real-time hazard alerts

These wearables connect to central AI platforms that issue alerts when:

- A worker enters a dangerous area

- Someone collapses due to heat or overexertion

- PPE is removed in restricted zones

4.8 AI for Safety Training and Simulations

AI is also improving **safety training** through:

- **VR-based hazard recognition training**

- **AI tutors** that quiz and adapt based on learning performance

- **Scenario simulations** based on real incidents

This method of **experiential learning** is more effective than lectures or manuals. Workers remember risks better when they "experience" them virtually.

4.9 AI and Emergency Response

AI systems also assist during active incidents:

- Use site cameras to track who's at risk

- Suggest **evacuation paths** based on crowd density and fire location

- Communicate automated alerts via SMS, wearables, or sirens

- Monitor air quality for chemical leaks or dust inhalation

Post-incident, AI analyzes response effectiveness to improve future protocols.

4.10 Real-World Example: Bechtel + Wearable AI

Bechtel integrated AI-driven wearables across large infrastructure projects. Results included:

- 35% reduction in near-miss incidents

- Faster emergency response time

- Improved compliance with safety walk-throughs

- Real-time tracking of workers during high-risk operations like welding and rigging

This data not only improved safety—it also helped with **insurance premiums**, as the firm could prove proactive risk management.

4.11 Predicting Environmental Hazards

Machine learning also helps detect and predict:

- **Heat stress** during high-temperature operations

- **Dust levels** at excavation zones

- **Noise levels** that could impair communication

- **Airborne contaminants** on demolition sites

AI platforms correlate weather, machinery output, and site activities to advise on when to stop work or change protective protocols.

4.12 Small Contractors and AI Safety Tools

AI safety is no longer reserved for mega-projects. Entry-level systems exist for small businesses:

- **Guardhat**: Smart safety wearables for construction

- **Modjoul**: AI-based safety dashboard and mobile alerts

- **Spot-r by Triax**: Location and motion sensors for workers

- **Caterpillar Vision AI**: Vehicle-based safety monitoring kits

Most systems offer plug-and-play options via mobile or tablet apps—no major tech setup needed.

4.13 Data Privacy and Ethics

While AI protects workers, it also introduces concerns:

- **Over-surveillance**: Workers may feel constantly watched

- **Bias**: AI models may wrongly flag certain individuals

- **Data use**: Who owns the health and activity data?

Firms must adopt **clear policies, transparency, and opt-in options** to earn trust and remain ethical.

AI safety should enhance freedom and protection—not create fear.

4.14 Workforce Culture Shift

AI-powered safety is most effective when paired with:

- **Worker buy-in**

- **Supervisor accountability**

- **Transparent data access**

- **Regular feedback loops**

Rather than being policed by machines, workers should feel **supported by smart systems**—as if a digital partner is watching their back.

4.15 Future Trends: Autonomous Safety Systems

Looking ahead, AI will bring:

- **Self-monitoring robots** patrolling sites for hazards

- **AI-controlled site gates** that deny access without safety compliance

- **Personal safety assistants** that whisper safety tips into smart helmets

- **AI-generated safety heatmaps** updated hourly by drone or CCTV

We're heading toward **zero-incident job sites**—where prevention is woven into every sensor, surface, and system.

Conclusion: Smarter, Safer, Stronger

AI is redefining safety and maintenance in construction. By catching failures and risks before they happen, it's saving time, money—and most importantly—lives.

The age of reactive firefighting is ending. With predictive machine learning, construction firms can:

- Prevent breakdowns

- Enhance safety culture

- Reduce insurance costs

- Improve compliance and morale

As we transition to **Chapter 5: AI-Driven Construction Robotics and Automation**, we'll explore how physical labor itself is being augmented—and in some cases, reimagined—by AI-powered robots.

Chapter 5: AI-Driven Construction Robotics and Automation

Introduction: The Rise of the Robotic Builder

Construction has long been seen as one of the most labor-intensive industries on Earth. From laying bricks and pouring concrete to climbing scaffolding and welding steel, the work is physically demanding, often dangerous, and dependent on skilled labor.

But what happens when machines not only assist but begin to autonomously perform core construction tasks?

Welcome to the new era of **AI-powered construction robotics**—where smart machines, guided by real-time data and machine learning algorithms, are revolutionizing how buildings are physically assembled.

This chapter unpacks the transformation from human-led labor to intelligent automation, and how construction sites are becoming **safer, faster, and more precise** thanks to robotics.

5.1 What Are Construction Robots?

Construction robots are autonomous or semi-autonomous machines that use AI, computer vision, and sensors to:

- **Perform physical tasks** like bricklaying, drilling, or painting

- **Navigate dynamic environments** (like uneven terrain or changing job sites)

- **Interact with humans and other machines**

- **Make decisions** based on real-time data (e.g., obstacle detection or material usage)

They vary in form and function:

- **Mobile robots** (like drones or wheeled bots)

- **Stationary arms** (for welding, assembly, 3D printing)

- **Wearable robotics** (exoskeletons enhancing human strength)

- **Hybrid robotic-human teams** (cobots)

AI is the brain. Robotics is the muscle. Together, they represent a fundamental shift in how we build.

5.2 Key Drivers Behind Robotic Adoption

Why are companies increasingly turning to AI-driven robots?

- **Labor shortages** in skilled trades

- **Rising safety standards** and regulatory pressure

- **Faster project timelines** demanded by clients

- **Repetitive task automation** freeing up human talent

- **Data-driven workflows** where machines adapt faster than people

These machines don't get tired, don't take breaks, and can operate in hazardous conditions—offering **consistency and precision unmatched by human labor alone**.

5.3 Real-World Examples of Construction Robotics

5.3.1 SAM100 – Semi-Automated Mason

SAM (Semi-Automated Mason) is a robotic bricklayer that can lay over **3,000 bricks per day**—3 to 5 times faster than a human, with uniform quality. Guided by computer vision and site maps, SAM adjusts for weather, wall deviations, and material changes in real time.

5.3.2 TyBot – Rebar Tying Robot

TyBot scans bridge decks and ties rebar autonomously, drastically reducing injuries in repetitive and laborious tying tasks. One operator can oversee multiple TyBots simultaneously.

5.3.3 Hadrian X – Bricklaying Robot by FBR

This Australian robot uses a 30-meter boom arm and laser-guided AI to place bricks with sub-millimeter precision. It can construct the walls of a house in under **48 hours** with minimal human assistance.

5.3.4 Boston Dynamics' Spot

This four-legged robot dog carries LiDAR scanners, thermal cameras, and 360° imaging tools to **inspect job sites, map progress**, and detect safety issues. It navigates stairs, mud, and complex terrain.

5.3.5 Exoskeletons – Human-Augmenting Robots

Powered suits from companies like **Ekso Bionics** and **Hilti** help workers lift heavy tools, reduce muscle strain, and minimize back injuries—especially for repetitive overhead tasks like drilling.

5.4 AI Makes Robots Smarter

While industrial robots have been around for decades, **AI is what unlocks their autonomy**. With machine learning and computer vision:

- Robots understand complex visual inputs (e.g., pipe locations or bolt alignment)

- Adapt to job site changes (e.g., wind, dust, human interference)

- Collaborate with humans via gestures, voice commands, or predictive positioning

- Improve over time by learning from outcomes

This creates a new generation of **adaptive and intelligent machines**, unlike the static robots of the factory floor.

5.5 Robotic Applications Across Construction Phases

AI-driven robotics is now present in almost every construction phase:

Design and Surveying

- **Drone-based mapping** with AI-generated topography and volume analysis

- **Autonomous rovers** that compare as-built conditions to digital plans

Foundation and Framing

- **3D-printed concrete foundations** created by large-scale robotic arms

- **Robots for steel cutting**, welding, and framing with laser precision

Enclosure and Finishing

- **Painting bots** with image recognition for edges, trims, and smooth coats

- **Tile-laying robots** that map floor dimensions and align patterns precisely

Maintenance and Post-Construction

- **Facade-cleaning robots** with AI-controlled suction and cleaning paths

- **Security and inspection bots** that monitor building health via AI diagnostics

5.6 Benefits of AI Robotics in Construction

5.6.1 Speed

Tasks that took weeks can now be completed in days. Robots don't need rest, and AI can optimize their routes and routines in real time.

5.6.2 Safety

Hazardous, high-risk tasks are performed by robots instead of humans—reducing accidents from falls, strains, or toxic exposures.

5.6.3 Precision

Robots execute tasks with micro-level accuracy, reducing rework, material waste, and cost overruns.

5.6.4 Cost Efficiency

Though the initial investment is high, long-term savings from reduced labor, downtime, and insurance claims often outweigh the cost.

5.6.5 Workforce Enhancement

Robots don't replace all labor—they augment it. Workers can supervise, troubleshoot, and handle creative or adaptive work instead of repetitive drudgery.

5.7 The Human-Robot Team: Cobots

Cobots (collaborative robots) are designed to work **side by side with humans**, sharing tools, workspace, and goals. Their AI is trained not just for efficiency—but also **for safety and responsiveness to human presence**.

Examples include:

- A cobot assisting with drywall by holding sheets in place

- A welding arm positioning materials while a human finishes details

- A painting bot adjusting spray angles based on worker feedback

This **symbiotic model** allows companies to benefit from the speed of robotics and the intuition of human workers simultaneously.

5.8 Challenges to Robotic Adoption

Despite rapid advancements, barriers remain:

- **High upfront cost** of robotic systems

- **Complex site navigation** in unpredictable environments

- **Limited fine-motor control** in highly detailed work

- **Regulatory hurdles** around autonomous machines on public sites

- **Worker resistance** due to fear of job loss

Overcoming these challenges requires:

- Transparent communication with labor teams

- Incremental rollout with training and integration

- Design of tasks that match robot strengths to human weaknesses

5.9 Small Firms and Modular Robotics

Robotics is often seen as accessible only to mega-contractors, but new **modular and rental models** are changing that.

Examples:

- **Dusty Robotics**: Offers layout-printing robots for small contractors

- **Rugged Robotics**: Leases layout bots to subcontractors for daily use

- **PaintJet**: Provides robotic painting as a service for mid-size developers

This "Robotics-as-a-Service" (RaaS) model lowers the barrier to entry—letting small players tap into automation without massive CapEx.

5.10 The Future: Fully Autonomous Construction Sites

Within the next decade, we may see:

- Entire walls 3D-printed by robots without formwork

- Autonomous cranes directed by AI-based sequencing engines

- Material delivery robots moving supplies across sites

- Robotic arms assembling modular components on scaffolds

- AI overseeing every inch of the site via drones and ground bots

These smart, data-rich ecosystems will continuously self-optimize—requiring minimal human intervention except for complex decision-making and oversight.

5.11 Ethical and Workforce Considerations

As with all automation, ethical questions arise:

- Will robots replace workers?

- Who is responsible for accidents caused by machines?

- Can AI-based robots be trusted with safety-critical tasks?

The answer lies in **re-skilling and job evolution**. Roles will shift toward:

- Robot supervision and maintenance

- AI system training and configuration

- Hybrid project management with digital fluency

Far from eliminating humans, robotics will **redefine human value** in construction—shifting from strength to strategy.

Conclusion: Reinventing the Workforce, Rebuilding the World

The rise of AI-powered robotics in construction isn't a far-off dream—it's happening now. Every year, robots become more mobile, more adaptive, and more collaborative.

For companies, this is a golden opportunity to:

- Boost productivity

- Enhance safety

- Lower costs

- Stay competitive in an evolving market

For workers, it's a call to evolve—to move from repetitive labor to high-value, tech-augmented roles.

In the next chapter, **Chapter 6: Supply Chain Optimization through AI**, we'll explore how artificial intelligence is transforming the invisible backbone of construction—materials, logistics, and inventory.

Chapter 6: Supply Chain Optimization through AI

Introduction: The Backbone of Every Build

A beautifully designed building, a skilled labor team, and state-of-the-art machinery mean little if your **cement hasn't arrived**, your steel is delayed, or your HVAC unit is stuck in customs. The supply chain is the lifeblood of construction—and often, its biggest pain point.

In a globalized industry where materials come from five continents and timelines are razor-thin, even minor disruptions can stall million-dollar projects. Enter **Artificial Intelligence**, which brings clarity, speed, and foresight to a supply system traditionally plagued by fragmentation, guesswork, and inefficiencies.

This chapter shows how AI is helping firms **predict demand**, **track inventory**, **prevent delays**, and **automate procurement**—transforming the supply chain into a competitive advantage rather than a bottleneck.

6.1 Understanding the Construction Supply Chain

A construction supply chain encompasses:

- **Procurement** of raw materials and finished components

- **Vendor selection** and contract management

- **Transportation and delivery logistics**

- **Inventory management** at warehouses or on-site

- **Material handling** and usage tracking

- **Waste reduction** and surplus resale

Each link involves multiple parties, often using separate systems. Delays, cost overruns, and miscommunication are common—and costly.

AI steps in to make sense of the **chaos**, connecting dots across time zones, currencies, transport modes, and shifting demand.

6.2 Key Challenges in Traditional Supply Chains

- **Lack of visibility** across vendors and delivery status

- **Inaccurate demand forecasting**

- **Over-ordering or under-ordering** materials

- **Manual procurement processes**

- **Delivery mismatches** or late shipments

- **Excess material waste** and storage issues

Many firms still use Excel sheets and verbal coordination to manage millions in supplies. In the era of AI, this is both inefficient and risky.

6.3 How AI Enhances Supply Chain Performance

AI solves these problems using:

- **Machine learning** to predict material needs

- **Natural language processing** to parse contracts and invoices

- **Computer vision** to track inventory

- **Predictive analytics** to model delivery delays

- **Autonomous systems** to reorder materials automatically

In short, AI transforms a reactive supply chain into a **proactive ecosystem**—alert, responsive, and resilient.

6.4 AI-Powered Demand Forecasting

One of AI's most powerful applications is **demand prediction**. Based on:

- BIM schedules

- Historical usage data

- Market prices and lead times

- Weather forecasts

- Project progress reports

AI tools generate **just-in-time (JIT)** material schedules that align precisely with project needs, reducing storage costs and delays.

For example, if drywall usage spikes during week 14 in similar projects, and a delay in framing occurs, the system postpones drywall ordering to week 16—automatically.

6.5 Smart Procurement and Vendor Optimization

AI helps firms:

- Evaluate vendor performance based on price, delivery time, and quality

- Automate RFQ generation and bidding analysis

- Identify at-risk suppliers early (e.g., political instability, shipping issues)

- Recommend alternate vendors based on real-time availability

- Negotiate smarter contracts using past data patterns

AI can even simulate **multi-vendor strategies** to reduce reliance on a single supplier and diversify risk.

6.6 Real-Time Tracking and Logistics Optimization

AI-enhanced GPS and IoT sensors allow:

- **Live tracking** of shipments, trucks, and containers

- **ETA predictions** based on traffic, weather, or customs delays

- **Route optimization** to avoid congestion or roadblocks

- **Cold-chain monitoring** for sensitive materials (e.g., adhesives, insulation)

- **Alert systems** for delays, theft, or damage en route

This ensures **materials arrive when needed, in perfect condition**, and with full traceability.

6.7 Inventory Management with AI

AI systems use:

- **Computer vision** to count materials via camera footage

- **Barcode and RFID scanning** for precise stock movement

- **Sensor data** to monitor storage conditions

- **Usage tracking** from digital tools to project depletion rates

They generate:

- **Live dashboards** for on-site supervisors

- **Reorder alerts** before stockouts occur

- **Waste analytics** to identify overuse or theft

- **Material balance reports** linked to BIM and accounting systems

This allows firms to **shrink surplus, prevent shortages**, and **automate restocking** with minimal oversight.

6.8 Autonomous and Robotic Material Handling

AI also enables **automated warehouses** and on-site delivery systems:

- **Autonomous forklifts** that transport materials to exact zones

- **Delivery drones** for light tools or documents

- **Mobile robots** that move pallets, rebar, or pipe

- **Digital twins** that simulate material flows for optimization

These reduce human errors, save time, and free up workers for skilled tasks.

6.9 Waste Reduction and Sustainability

Construction generates **one-third of global waste**. AI helps combat this by:

- **Predicting material surplus** before orders are placed

- **Recommending recycled or eco-friendly substitutes**

- **Flagging wasteful practices** by comparing actual vs. planned usage

- **Connecting surplus to resale marketplaces**

Sustainability and profit no longer conflict—with AI, they align.

6.10 Case Study: AI in Action – Skanska

Skanska implemented an AI-driven supply chain system on a major U.S. healthcare project:

- AI predicted delivery bottlenecks 12 days in advance

- Suggested alternate vendors when drywall supplier reported delays

- Cut material waste by **18%**

- Improved delivery accuracy by **22%**

- Reduced on-site storage costs by **30%**

AI turned a complex supply web into a responsive nervous system—anticipating problems before they became crises.

6.11 Platforms Driving AI Supply Chain Innovation

- **Kewazo** – AI + robotics for autonomous scaffolding material transport

- **Giatec Smart Concrete Sensors** – Optimize concrete curing and mix schedules

- **Buildots** – AI cameras track material installation vs. BIM

- **SmartPM** – AI-integrated project scheduling and procurement insights

- **CONXAI** – AI insights from construction workflows for logistics teams

These tools bring visibility and automation to what was once manual, opaque, and chaotic.

6.12 Challenges to AI Supply Chain Adoption

- **Data inconsistency** across vendors and departments

- **Legacy systems** resistant to integration

- **Short-term mindset** avoiding tech investment

- **Cybersecurity risks** of connected systems

- **Need for human oversight** despite automation

Adoption requires **digital literacy, leadership vision**, and **a shift from spreadsheets to systems thinking**.

6.13 AI for Small and Medium Contractors

You don't need a massive budget to benefit. Affordable AI tools exist:

- **Fonn** – Project tracking and logistics for SMEs

- **Tradify** – AI-driven scheduling and supply coordination

- **Buildxact** – Estimates and inventory forecasting for residential builders

- **MaterialBank** – AI-assisted sourcing for design materials

Even **WhatsApp bots** integrated with AI are helping contractors in emerging markets track deliveries and manage vendors.

6.14 Human Roles in an AI Supply Chain

AI doesn't replace supply chain managers—it **amplifies them**. Future roles include:

- AI interpreter and exception manager

- Vendor performance analyst

- Sustainability sourcing specialist

- Digital procurement strategist

Humans focus on **ethics, creativity, relationships**, and **strategy**—while AI handles the grunt work and pattern recognition.

Conclusion: From Chaos to Coordination

Construction's supply chain is no longer an unpredictable tangle of trucks, quotes, and warehouses. With AI, it becomes a **synchronized system**—where decisions are faster, deliveries are smarter, and materials flow like clockwork.

The gains are real:

- Fewer project delays

- Leaner inventory

- Reduced waste

- Lower costs

- Better vendor relationships

As we move forward to **Chapter 7: AI in Structural Engineering and Quality Control**, we'll examine how AI not only helps build—but ensures every beam and bolt meets the highest standards of integrity.

Chapter 7: AI in Structural Engineering and Quality Control

Introduction: Engineering Beyond the Human Limit

Structural engineering lies at the very core of construction—ensuring that every beam, column, and joint can withstand the forces of gravity, wind, earthquakes, and time. It's where mathematics meets material, and failure is not an option.

For decades, engineers have relied on finite element analysis (FEA), hand calculations, and their experience. But even the best minds can only account for a limited number of variables at once.

Enter AI.

With vast computing power and real-time data processing, AI is now enhancing the work of engineers—**detecting hidden flaws**, **modeling complex stress patterns**, and **ensuring structural safety** like never before. This chapter explores how AI is

reinforcing the very backbone of our built
environment.

7.1 The Role of Structural Engineering in Construction

Structural engineering is the discipline that ensures buildings and infrastructure can:

- Withstand loads (live, dead, seismic, wind, etc.)

- Resist corrosion, fatigue, and material degradation

- Comply with safety codes and design standards

- Maintain structural integrity over time

Every construction project involves a delicate balance between:

- Strength and flexibility

- Cost and material efficiency

- Aesthetic and load-bearing functions

AI helps optimize these trade-offs by crunching numbers, modeling stress paths, and simulating scenarios that would take humans weeks or months.

7.2 How AI Supports Structural Design

AI doesn't replace engineers—it **augments** their insight with computational speed and data depth.

Capabilities include:

- Analyzing multiple design variants for cost and stability

- Modeling complex geometries like curves, cantilevers, and shell structures

- Performing early-stage feasibility checks based on site and material parameters

- Identifying overdesigned or under-reinforced areas

- Predicting failure points under extreme stress or environmental conditions

AI enables a **shift from empirical design to data-driven design**.

7.3 AI in Finite Element Analysis (FEA)

FEA is the simulation of physical behavior under stress by breaking a structure into discrete elements. AI improves FEA by:

- **Speeding up calculations** through neural networks trained on previous simulations

- **Predicting material performance** under complex conditions

- **Suggesting reinforcement adjustments** to meet load targets

- **Visualizing stress paths** in 3D with real-time feedback

Startups like **nTopology**, **Altair**, and **Ansys AI** integrate machine learning to enhance FEA outputs—cutting analysis time from hours to minutes.

7.4 Smart Materials and AI Sensors

AI extends engineering beyond design—into **monitoring and maintenance** using smart materials and embedded sensors:

- **Strain gauges** embedded in beams transmit deformation data

- **Fiber optic sensors** detect cracks or shifts within concrete

- **Vibration sensors** assess resonance and structural fatigue

- **Temperature and moisture sensors** flag environmental stress

AI processes this data to:

- Detect micro-fractures before visible damage

- Predict long-term deterioration

- Trigger alerts for structural inspections

- Simulate wear and tear years in advance

This turns passive structures into **self-monitoring assets**.

7.5 Generative Structural Design

Using AI, engineers can input:

- Load conditions

- Space constraints

- Material choices

- Budget limits

And generate **thousands of structural solutions**, each evaluated for:

- Load-bearing performance

- Cost-efficiency

- Sustainability

- Buildability

This is known as **generative structural design**, and tools like **Spacemaker AI**, **Hypar**, and **Autodesk Forma** make it possible to explore designs previously unthinkable due to complexity or computation limits.

7.6 Structural Health Monitoring (SHM) with AI

SHM systems continuously monitor the condition of structures like:

- Bridges

- Dams

- High-rise buildings

- Stadiums

- Tunnels

AI enhances SHM by:

- **Detecting anomalies** (e.g., abnormal stress patterns) in real time

- **Classifying damage severity** using historical patterns

- **Predicting life-cycle degradation** to guide maintenance

- **Correlating sensor readings with external factors** (traffic, earthquakes, weather)

These insights help reduce catastrophic failures and enable **predictive maintenance schedules**.

7.7 AI for Code Compliance and Design Validation

AI tools assist engineers in:

- Verifying compliance with building codes (e.g., Eurocode, ACI, IS codes)

- Automating checks on reinforcement ratios, slab thickness, column spacing

- Flagging mismatches between architectural and structural plans

- Validating designs before submission for permitting

Some platforms even **generate code-annotated design reports** ready for regulatory approval—cutting down documentation time significantly.

7.8 Computer Vision for Quality Control

Computer vision systems powered by AI use images and videos to:

- Verify proper placement of rebars, bolts, and joints

- Detect cracks, voids, and material inconsistencies

- Assess curing of concrete via surface texture

- Confirm as-built accuracy vs. plans

Systems like **Buildots**, **OpenSpace**, and **DroneDeploy AI** capture thousands of daily images across the site and flag potential defects—long before human inspectors would notice.

7.9 Drone and Laser Scanning for Structural Checks

AI-enabled drones perform:

- 3D laser scanning (LiDAR) of structural frames

- Roof and facade inspection for warping or sagging

- Thermal imaging to detect leaks or weak spots

- Progress tracking against BIM models

This not only speeds up inspections but also provides **digital twins**—high-fidelity digital replicas used for simulation and lifecycle tracking.

7.10 Case Study: AI and Engineering at Arup

Arup, one of the world's leading engineering firms, used AI and parametric modeling to:

- Optimize truss patterns in the **Sydney Opera House roof renovation**

- Reduce steel usage in high-rise structural frames by 12%

- Create custom AI models for dynamic wind load analysis

By integrating AI with their existing engineering workflows, Arup enhanced both **aesthetic expression and structural reliability**.

7.11 Enhancing Safety Through Structural AI

Structural collapses, though rare, are devastating. AI helps prevent them by:

- Modeling **progressive collapse scenarios**

- Analyzing **load redistribution** in failure states

- Suggesting **redundant load paths**

- Assessing **real-time stress changes** during construction (e.g., formwork removal)

AI doesn't just check if a structure *can* hold—it ensures it can continue to do so *even if something goes wrong.*

7.12 Limitations and Human Oversight

AI is a powerful assistant—but structural safety still requires human:

- Judgment

- Experience

- Ethics

- Creativity

Engineers must validate AI outputs, especially when lives are at stake. The best results come from a **hybrid approach**—where machines compute, and humans contextualize.

7.13 Small Firms Using AI for Engineering

You don't need to be a global firm to use AI in engineering. Affordable tools include:

- **SkyCiv** – Cloud-based structural analysis with AI plugins

- **IDEA StatiCa** – Joint and connection analysis with design checks

- **ClearCalcs** – AI-assisted beam, footing, and column calculators for SMEs

- **Tally** – LCA (life cycle assessment) tools for sustainable engineering

These tools make structural AI accessible to small contractors, consultancies, and solo engineers.

7.14 The Future: AI-Centric Engineering Workflows

In coming years, AI will enable:

- **Real-time simulation during design**

- **AI co-pilots for structural engineers** suggesting reinforcements or materials

- **Automated clash detection across structural and MEP systems**

- **Self-optimizing frames** that adapt based on live loads or earthquakes

- **AI-curated design libraries** personalized to each engineer's past work

Engineering will become **fluid, intelligent, and interactive**—combining science with machine intuition.

Conclusion: From Steel to Silicon

Structural engineering is entering a new era—one where algorithms reinforce our intuition, and data replaces assumption. AI enables buildings to be:

- Stronger

- Safer

- Leaner

- Smarter

As we advance to **Chapter 8: Sustainability and Green Building with Artificial Intelligence**, we'll explore how AI is making construction not only efficient—but also *responsible*, guiding us

Chapter 8: Sustainability and Green Building with Artificial Intelligence

Introduction: Building for Tomorrow, Starting Today

Construction accounts for nearly **40% of global carbon emissions**, including energy used in buildings and the embodied carbon in materials. The industry has long been criticized for its wasteful practices, high energy usage, and reliance on non-renewable resources.

But a transformation is underway.

With the rise of climate-conscious policies, sustainable certifications (like LEED, BREEAM, WELL), and public demand for green infrastructure, the pressure is mounting to make construction **cleaner, smarter, and more sustainable**.

And Artificial Intelligence is emerging as a **crucial enabler** of this transition.

In this chapter, we explore how AI is helping construction firms reduce their environmental footprint—through smarter design, efficient operations, circular building practices, and predictive modeling for sustainability.

8.1 Understanding Green Building

A green building is designed and built to:

- Minimize energy and water consumption

- Use sustainable or recycled materials

- Reduce waste during and after construction

- Improve indoor environmental quality

- Lower overall carbon footprint

- Adapt to climate change and support biodiversity

Green construction doesn't just benefit the planet—it reduces costs over the building's lifecycle and enhances health, well-being, and long-term asset value.

AI acts as a catalyst—**automating, optimizing, and accelerating** every green decision.

8.2 The Urgency of Sustainable Construction

The World Green Building Council warns that to meet the 1.5°C climate target:

- All new buildings must be **net-zero carbon** by 2030

- Existing buildings must be **retrofitted** at scale

- Material use must shift toward **low-carbon alternatives**

AI helps achieve these goals by offering **real-time environmental insights, carbon footprint modeling**, and **data-driven sustainability planning**.

8.3 AI in Sustainable Design and Simulation

During the design phase, AI tools can:

- Optimize building orientation for natural light and ventilation

- Simulate **daylight autonomy**, glare risk, and shading impact

- Calculate energy usage across different seasons

- Recommend sustainable materials with lower embodied carbon

- Assess design compliance with green certification standards

Tools like **ClimateStudio**, **Sefaira**, and **Tally** allow architects and engineers to **simulate environmental performance** before construction begins—saving time, cost, and emissions.

Example: AI might suggest rotating the building by 17° to reduce annual HVAC energy by 22%.

8.4 Energy Efficiency with AI

AI-enabled energy models monitor and predict:

- Heating, cooling, and ventilation needs

- Occupancy patterns and lighting usage

- Solar panel output and battery storage

- HVAC system efficiency and anomaly detection

Smart energy management systems adjust conditions in real time—reducing unnecessary energy use while maintaining comfort.

AI can also:

- Autonomously control blinds, windows, and lighting based on daylight

- Recommend energy-saving retrofits based on usage data

- Simulate the ROI of energy-efficient technologies

8.5 Material Optimization and Embodied Carbon Tracking

Embodied carbon includes all emissions from mining, processing, transport, and manufacturing of materials. AI helps reduce this by:

- **Optimizing structural geometry** to use less concrete or steel

- Suggesting **recycled or local materials** to reduce transportation emissions

- Using databases like EC3 or OneClickLCA to select low-carbon options

- Forecasting **waste volumes** from each material type and proposing reuse options

For example, AI might recommend using geopolymer concrete instead of OPC, reducing carbon by 70%.

8.6 Waste Reduction with AI

Construction generates **2.2 billion tons of waste** annually. AI-powered tools reduce this by:

- Predicting over-ordering based on past projects

- Flagging on-site material misuse

- Optimizing cut lengths and shapes to reduce offcuts

- Monitoring dumpsters with cameras and sensors

- Connecting surplus materials to local reuse or resale networks

AI makes waste **visible**, **trackable**, and **preventable**—enabling leaner, cleaner operations.

8.7 Circular Construction and Deconstruction AI

Circular construction focuses on **designing for disassembly**, reuse, and minimal resource input. AI helps by:

- Tagging reusable materials with digital IDs and QR codes

- Planning demolition sequences that preserve valuable components

- Mapping material flows across building lifecycles

- Suggesting deconstruction strategies vs. demolition

Firms like **Madaster** and **BAMB** use AI to create **"material passports"**, ensuring that today's building can become tomorrow's resource.

8.8 Smart Water Management with AI

AI-powered systems optimize water use by:

- Predicting occupancy-based water demand

- Detecting leaks in plumbing systems via flow anomalies

- Automating irrigation based on weather forecasts

- Recommending water-saving appliances or fixtures

- Monitoring graywater systems for reuse efficiency

This reduces both **water waste** and **energy required to pump, heat, or treat water**.

8.9 Green Certifications and AI Assistance

AI accelerates the green building certification process by:

- Automating documentation for LEED, BREEAM, WELL, etc.

- Verifying compliance via digital twin comparisons

- Flagging design elements that reduce points (e.g., glare, ventilation imbalance)

- Suggesting changes to maximize rating performance

This reduces the **cost, time, and complexity** of sustainable certification—especially for mid-size firms.

8.10 AI for Climate Resilience and Adaptation

Sustainability also means **resilience**. AI helps assess and improve resilience to:

- Flooding and storm surges via terrain analysis

- Wildfires through vegetation and heat simulations

- Earthquakes with structural modeling and risk mapping

- Heatwaves via urban heat island reduction strategies

AI tools model **site-specific risk scenarios**, enabling climate-smart design that can withstand extreme events.

8.11 AI and Carbon Offsetting

Beyond reducing emissions, AI also supports carbon offsetting by:

- Calculating residual emissions of projects

- Recommending certified offset programs (e.g., reforestation, renewables)

- Verifying offset integrity using satellite imagery and blockchain

- Helping firms plan toward **net-zero construction goals**

This ensures environmental impact is minimized across the **entire project lifecycle**, not just the construction phase.

8.12 Case Study: Edge Technologies (Amsterdam)

The Edge building in Amsterdam, developed by OVG and designed by PLP, is considered one of the **smartest and greenest buildings in the world**. AI systems control:

- HVAC based on desk occupancy

- Lighting based on weather and circadian rhythm

- Energy balance via solar panels and battery systems

- Maintenance alerts from embedded IoT sensors

It consumes **70% less energy** than similar-sized buildings and achieved **BREEAM Outstanding** certification.

8.13 AI and Urban Sustainability

AI goes beyond individual buildings to:

- Optimize **urban layout** for sunlight and airflow

- Simulate **traffic and mobility** impacts of new developments

- Forecast **energy demand** for entire districts

- Guide **green infrastructure** placement (trees, water bodies, bioswales)

Tools like **CityFormLab**, **Sidewalk Labs**, and **UrbanFootprint** use AI to **reimagine sustainable cities**, not just buildings.

8.14 Barriers to AI in Green Construction

Challenges include:

- Limited data availability for accurate simulation

- Resistance to change from traditional practices

- Higher upfront costs despite long-term savings

- Integration issues with legacy building systems

- Need for training in AI-enhanced sustainability tools

These can be overcome through **policy incentives**, **client education**, and **interdisciplinary collaboration**.

8.15 Empowering Small Firms and Contractors

Even small firms can implement AI-driven sustainability with tools like:

- **Tally** – Life-cycle assessment for Revit users

- **cove.tool** – Real-time performance modeling for architecture firms

- **Autodesk Insight** – Cloud-based energy analysis

- **Green Building Studio** – AI modeling for MEP systems

- **EC3** – Free embodied carbon database for procurement teams

These tools democratize green building—bringing sustainability within reach of everyone.

Conclusion: A Greener Blueprint with AI

AI is not just helping us build faster and cheaper—it's helping us build better. With intelligent systems guiding every decision, construction can become:

- Cleaner

- More efficient

- More ethical

- Planet-positive

Green building is no longer a luxury or trend. It's a necessity. And with AI, it's finally practical—scalable, automated, and powerful.

As we move to **Chapter 9: Legal, Ethical, and Workforce Impacts of AI in Construction**, we will explore how this technological transformation is reshaping job roles, legal frameworks, and the ethics of building in an AI-driven world.

Chapter 9: Legal, Ethical, and Workforce Impacts of AI in Construction

Introduction: The Human Side of the Algorithm

Artificial Intelligence is transforming how we design, build, monitor, and maintain infrastructure. But with every new tool and advancement comes a deeper set of questions:

- What happens to human jobs when robots can build walls?

- Who is responsible if an AI makes a critical error?

- Can a machine be trusted to inspect a structure, enforce codes, or decide safety priorities?

- What about surveillance, data privacy, and consent on job sites?

This chapter addresses the **legal responsibilities**, **ethical dilemmas**, and **workforce disruptions** that AI introduces into construction—issues that cannot be solved by software alone.

9.1 The Changing Nature of Labor in Construction

AI and robotics are reshaping the roles of workers across every stage of construction:

Traditional Roles at Risk of Automation

- Manual laborers for repetitive tasks (e.g., bricklaying, painting, rebar tying)

- Surveyors and estimators relying on manual data collection

- Schedule planners using static spreadsheets

- On-site inspectors performing routine quality checks

Emerging AI-Augmented Roles

- Drone operators and site data analysts

- AI model trainers and algorithm supervisors

- Robotics technicians and maintainers

- Digital twin architects and simulation experts

- Human-AI collaboration managers (a new breed of site supervisor)

Rather than complete job loss, AI brings **job transformation**. Labor evolves from muscle to mind, from routine to strategic.

9.2 Reskilling and Workforce Development

The construction sector must urgently address the **AI skills gap** by investing in:

- **Technical training programs** for digital tools, BIM, and AI interfaces

- **Cross-disciplinary learning** between engineering, IT, and field operations

- **Certifications in AI-enhanced construction systems**

- **Apprenticeships in AI-supported workflows** for tradespeople

Without structured reskilling programs, workers risk being displaced—not by AI itself, but by the lack of support to transition into new roles.

Governments, unions, and companies must cooperate to build an **inclusive digital workforce**.

9.3 Labor Rights in an Automated Site

AI also raises new questions about:

- **Worker surveillance** (via wearables, cameras, and AI tools)

- **Algorithmic decision-making** affecting task assignments or productivity scoring

- **Data ownership** of biometric and behavioral metrics collected on job sites

Clear policies are needed to:

- Protect worker privacy

- Provide transparency in AI decision-making

- Establish grievance mechanisms for algorithmic errors or bias

- Ensure consent before collecting sensitive data

Ethical AI in construction must put **people first—even on a robot-rich site**.

9.4 Legal Liability and AI Errors

Who is responsible if:

- An AI-powered drone crashes and injures someone?

- A robotic bricklayer builds a wall that later collapses?

- An AI system fails to detect a structural defect?

Legal frameworks currently assume **human accountability**—but AI blurs that line.

New models of liability may include:

- **Shared responsibility** between developer, operator, and AI vendor

- **AI insurance policies** covering autonomous systems

- **Mandated human oversight** in safety-critical decisions

- **Fail-safe protocols** and system transparency requirements

Courts and legal professionals must develop **standards of due care** in AI-guided operations.

9.5 Data Governance and Privacy

AI thrives on data—much of it sensitive, including:

- Worker movements and biometrics

- Site imagery and proprietary design files

- Client specifications and cost breakdowns

This introduces risks of:

- **Data breaches** or leaks of confidential plans

- **Misuse** of facial recognition or GPS tracking

- **Unauthorized data sale** to third-party analytics firms

Regulations like **GDPR**, **CCPA**, and emerging **AI Acts** require:

- Consent-based data collection

- Transparency in usage

- Security protocols and data anonymization

- Right to access or delete personal data

Construction firms must integrate **cybersecurity and data ethics** into their AI strategies.

9.6 Bias and Fairness in AI Decision-Making

If AI is trained on biased data, it can reinforce inequality in:

- Hiring or task allocation

- Performance ratings

- Safety violation detection (e.g., disproportionately flagging certain groups)

- Vendor selection and procurement scoring

To mitigate this, AI systems must be:

- Trained on **diverse and representative datasets**

- Audited for **algorithmic bias**

- Designed with **explainability and human review loops**

- Governed by **inclusive stakeholder policies**

AI should not only avoid harm—it should **actively promote fairness and equity** on job sites.

9.7 Intellectual Property and Automation

As AI starts generating designs, layouts, schedules, and even full project simulations, legal ownership becomes unclear:

- Who owns an AI-generated BIM model?

- Can an AI-designed structure be copyrighted?

- Is the design firm or software provider the legal creator?

Emerging legal interpretations suggest:

- The **human directing the AI** retains authorship

- Contractual terms should define ownership in collaborative AI use

- AI outputs must meet originality criteria for copyright protection

Legal clarity will become crucial as **AI creativity blurs authorship lines**.

9.8 Regulation and AI Governance in Construction

Governments and industry bodies are beginning to draft policies on:

- Autonomous machinery usage on construction sites

- AI-based inspections and digital permitting

- Environmental impact reporting using AI systems

- Workplace AI ethics codes

Examples:

- **EU AI Act** – Categorizes AI systems by risk and mandates safety, transparency

- **ISO 37106 & 19650** – Standards for smart construction and BIM

- **Smart Cities charters** – Define responsible use of urban AI infrastructure

Construction leaders must stay ahead of these evolving **legal and compliance requirements** to avoid penalties and reputational harm.

9.9 Union and Worker Advocacy in the AI Era

Labor unions must evolve too—negotiating for:

- **AI oversight rights**

- **Fair distribution of productivity gains** (e.g., profit-sharing from automation)

- **Mandatory training and upskilling programs**

- **Worker representation in AI procurement decisions**

Instead of resisting change, unions can help **shape the ethical use of AI**, ensuring workers benefit from technological advancement.

9.10 Case Study: Skanska and AI Ethics Charter

Skanska, a global construction firm, established an internal AI Ethics Charter with principles like:

- All AI must be **human-centric**

- Worker data use requires **transparency and consent**

- AI must be **explainable and auditable**

- Safety-critical AI must always include **human-in-the-loop decisions**

By embedding ethics into its AI strategy, Skanska builds trust—with workers, regulators, and clients alike.

9.11 The Role of Legal Professionals and Compliance Officers

As AI use grows, legal and compliance professionals will need:

- Familiarity with **AI technologies** and data science basics

- Ability to interpret **emerging AI regulations**

- Tools to conduct **AI impact assessments**

- Frameworks for **risk mitigation and dispute resolution** involving AI systems

They will serve as **guardians of responsible automation**, ensuring that innovation does not outpace accountability.

9.12 Building a Responsible AI Culture

The most important shift is not technological—but cultural. Construction firms must:

- Foster **interdisciplinary collaboration** between engineers, ethicists, lawyers, and AI developers

- Create **AI governance boards**

- Conduct **ethics workshops and scenario planning**

- Encourage **whistleblower protections** for AI misuse

- Celebrate **AI use cases that improve worker wellbeing**, not just profits

A strong ethical foundation today ensures that the **AI-powered construction industry of tomorrow is just, inclusive, and sustainable**.

Conclusion: Rights, Risks, and Responsibility

AI is not just another tool—it is a force that reshapes power dynamics, decision-making, and responsibility. In construction, where every decision can impact lives, we must wield AI **not just with intelligence—but with wisdom**.

The future of construction will be defined not only by how well we build—but by **how ethically and equitably we deploy the tools of building**.

As we move to the final chapter—**Chapter 10: The Future of Construction: AI-Powered Smart Cities and Beyond**—we'll explore how these technologies converge at scale, building intelligent urban environments that respond to their inhabitants in real time.

Chapter 10: The Future of Construction: AI-Powered Smart Cities and Beyond

Introduction: From Buildings to Living Cities

Over the last nine chapters, we've seen how AI revolutionizes the construction industry—enhancing design, planning, safety, structural integrity, sustainability, and even ethics. But now, we widen our lens.

What happens when AI isn't just applied to a building—but to a **whole city**?

Welcome to the era of **smart cities**—urban environments where roads, buildings, infrastructure, and services are interconnected, data-driven, and guided by intelligent systems. And at the core of this transformation lies the **construction industry**—the engineers and builders crafting the physical backbone of this digital revolution.

This chapter takes us into the near future, where **AI-built cities don't just shelter**

us—they serve, adapt, and evolve with us.

10.1 Defining Smart Cities

A **smart city** uses digital technologies—including AI, IoT, 5G, big data, and robotics—to:

- Improve urban services (transport, water, power, healthcare)

- Reduce environmental impact

- Enhance citizen engagement

- Increase safety and mobility

- Optimize infrastructure efficiency

Construction is the starting point for all of it. Smart cities are **built smart**, not just **run smart**.

10.2 Construction's Role in Smart City Development

AI guides the planning, design, and execution of smart city infrastructure by:

- **Optimizing site selection** using geospatial and demographic data

- **Designing mixed-use, walkable zones** through simulation

- **Embedding sensors** into roads, buildings, and utilities during construction

- **Enabling modular and prefabricated housing** with robotic assembly

- **Ensuring sustainability targets** are met at scale

In short, builders become the **coders of urban reality**, laying the digital fabric beneath every sidewalk and skyscraper.

10.3 Digital Twins and AI-Driven Urban Planning

Digital twins are virtual models of real-world environments—bridges, hospitals, parks, entire neighborhoods—updated in real time via sensors and data feeds.

AI uses digital twins to:

- Simulate traffic flows and pedestrian safety

- Forecast infrastructure stress under population growth

- Model energy consumption across districts

- Predict flood zones or urban heat island effects

- Optimize emergency response routing

Cities like Singapore, Shanghai, and Dubai already use AI-based twins to guide zoning, emergency drills, and resource allocation.

10.4 AI in Urban Infrastructure Construction

AI is used to:

- Design **adaptive roads** that self-report potholes and redirect traffic

- Optimize placement of **renewable energy microgrids**

- Construct **modular hospitals** with AI-based capacity forecasting

- Enable **autonomous drone lanes** for medical deliveries or inspections

- Lay **intelligent water pipes** that detect and fix leaks

The future isn't just smart buildings—it's a smart **fabric** of connected, self-healing infrastructure.

10.5 Smart Housing and Prefabricated AI Design

To solve urban housing crises, AI aids:

- Rapid design of affordable units using generative algorithms

- Robotic prefabrication for walls, modules, and components

- On-site assembly by AI-guided cranes and bots

- Predictive maintenance systems embedded in homes

- AI voice assistants integrated into building systems

Homes will be **designed by AI**, **built by machines**, and **run by data**—improving affordability, energy efficiency, and accessibility.

10.6 AI-Enhanced Urban Mobility Systems

Construction firms now help create:

- Roads that interact with self-driving vehicles

- AI-controlled traffic lights that reduce congestion

- Adaptive sidewalks for pedestrians, bikes, and delivery bots

- Smart parking lots that guide cars to open spots

- Intermodal hubs connecting buses, trains, and micromobility in real time

Mobility infrastructure becomes **data-responsive**, minimizing emissions and delays while maximizing access.

10.7 Environmental Intelligence and Urban Resilience

In future cities, AI monitors and responds to:

- **Air quality and emissions** using sensor networks

- **Green space balance** to combat heat islands

- **Stormwater flows** to prevent flooding

- **Noise levels** for zoning enforcement

- **Wildlife tracking** to preserve ecosystems

Construction professionals must now build with **ecological foresight**, using AI to create **nature-integrated urban forms**.

10.8 Ethics and Equity in Smart Cities

As cities become smarter, **ethical design** is more important than ever. AI must be used to:

- Ensure **equitable access** to smart infrastructure

- Avoid digital redlining or biased surveillance

- Protect data privacy and autonomy

- Preserve cultural identity amid technological change

- Empower citizens to **co-design** their neighborhoods

Construction professionals will play a key role in implementing **human-centered, inclusive urbanism**.

10.9 Case Study: NEOM, Saudi Arabia

NEOM is a $500B city under construction in Saudi Arabia, designed to be:

- **AI-managed** from streetlights to food supply chains

- **Car-free and carbon-neutral**

- Featuring **The Line**: a 170km-long, 200m-wide linear city

- Constructed with **robotic labor**, **modular structures**, and **3D printing**

NEOM's vision highlights how **AI-driven design meets bold political will**, and how construction is evolving from building structures to **creating ecosystems**.

10.10 AI in Post-Construction Life Cycle Management

Construction doesn't end when a building opens. AI continues to:

- Predict and schedule maintenance needs

- Optimize energy use based on occupancy

- Guide retrofitting based on wear-and-tear

- Track material performance for future recycling

- Alert authorities to safety risks or damage

AI ensures cities remain **healthy and operational**—well beyond day one.

10.11 The Rise of the Construction Technologist

As we move into this smart era, a new kind of professional emerges:

- Fluent in BIM, AI, data science, and robotics

- Skilled in sustainable design and digital twins

- Comfortable across physical and virtual environments

- Able to **coordinate machines, people, and policies**

This "construction technologist" blends **engineering, coding, and urban strategy**—building not just structures, but societies.

10.12 Education and Policy for a Smart Construction Future

To build AI-powered cities, we must invest in:

- **Curriculum reform** in architecture, engineering, and trade schools

- **Public-private innovation hubs** focused on urban AI

- **Open-data standards** for construction platforms

- **Incentives** for green, AI-guided development

- **Citizen engagement platforms** for urban feedback loops

The smart city is not just a tech product—it's a **civic partnership**.

Conclusion: The City That Thinks, the Builder Who Leads

We are entering an era where cities will:

- Think in real time

- Adapt to climate and community

- Heal themselves

- Empower people to live more freely, sustainably, and beautifully

And all of it begins with construction—the humble act of building, reimagined through the lens of AI.

As builders, architects, planners, and leaders, we are not just creating walls and roads—we are shaping the **destinies of nations and the future of humanity**.

Let us build not only with concrete, but with **conscience**. Not only with speed, but with **wisdom**. And not only with profit in mind, but with **purpose in heart**.

The age of AI in construction is not ahead of us—it is **already here**.

Let's build the future. Intelligently. Ethically.
Together.

Acknowledgments

This book would not have been possible without the wisdom, encouragement, and vision of the many individuals and communities who continue to reshape the built world with intelligence and heart.

To the pioneering engineers, architects, urban planners, technologists, and laborers who are embracing AI to construct not just smarter structures but better societies—your innovation is our inspiration.

Special thanks to the educators and mentors who push the boundaries of construction knowledge; the startups and software pioneers redefining what's possible; and the global community of builders, coders, and thinkers dedicated to sustainable and ethical development.

Above all, heartfelt gratitude to **Arpita Arya**, whose brilliance, grace, and unwavering drive continue to light the path ahead.

Thank you for believing that the future can—and must—be built better.

Glossary

- **AI (Artificial Intelligence):** Computer systems that simulate human intelligence tasks like learning, problem-solving, and decision-making.

- **BIM (Building Information Modeling):** A 3D modeling process used in design, planning, and construction.

- **Digital Twin:** A real-time digital replica of a physical structure, system, or process.

- **Generative Design:** AI-powered design exploration that creates optimized building solutions based on constraints.

- **IoT (Internet of Things):** Interconnected devices that collect and share data over the internet.

- **Machine Learning:** A subset of AI that enables computers to learn from data and improve over time without explicit programming.

- **Modular Construction:**
  Pre-fabricated building components assembled on-site.

- **Predictive Maintenance:**
  AI-enabled system that forecasts machinery breakdowns before they happen.

- **Smart Cities:** Urban areas that use AI, data, and connectivity to optimize services and infrastructure.

- **Sustainability:** Building practices that minimize environmental impact and promote long-term resource use.

Index

About the Author

Sayeed Siddiqui is a technology futurist, certified cybersecurity expert (CISSP), and lifelong learner dedicated to exploring the intersection of artificial intelligence, sustainability, and human progress. With a passion for transforming traditional industries through innovation, he has authored books on AI's impact across healthcare, finance, media, defense, law, and logistics.

His unique ability to simplify complex technologies makes his writing both practical and inspiring. As a poet, strategist, and advocate for ethical AI, Sayeed believes that technology must uplift, include, and humanize every profession it touches.

He can be reached at **supreme.clarion@gmail.com**.

www.ingramcontent.com/pod-product-compliance
Lightning Source LLC
LaVergne TN
LVHW022343060326
832902LV00022B/4208